D0622858

Little
Pebble™

Construction Vehicles at Work

DUMP TRUCKS

by Kathryn Clay

CAPSTONE PRESS
a capstone imprint

Little Pebble is published by Capstone Press,
1710 Roe Crest Drive, North Mankato, Minnesota 56003
www.mycapstone.com

Library of Congress Cataloging-in-Publication Data
Names: Clay, Kathryn, author.
Title: Dump trucks / by Kathryn Clay.
Description: North Mankato, Minnesota : Capstone Press, [2017] | Series:
   Little pebble. Construction vehicles at work | Audience: Ages 4–8 |
   Audience: K to grade 3 | Includes bibliographical references and index.
Identifiers: LCCN 2015048724| ISBN 9781515725268 (library binding) |
ISBN 9781515725305 (pbk.) | ISBN 9781515725367 (ebook pdf)
Subjects: LCSH: Dump trucks—Juvenile literature.
Classification: LCC TL230 .C53 2017 | DDC 629.224—dc23
LC record available at http://lccn.loc.gov/2015048724

Editorial Credits
Erika L. Shores, editor; Juliette Peters and Kayla Rossow, designers;
Eric Gohl, media researcher; Tori Abraham, production specialist

Photo Credits
iStockphoto: amysuem, 19, kozmoat98, 5, 7; Shutterstock: Chris VanLennep Photo, 11, Faraways, 13, GIRODJL, cover, Johan Larson, 1, sondem, 17, TFoxFoto, 9, 15, Thomas Riggins, 21

Design elements: Shutterstock

Printed in China.
007704

Table of Contents

About Dump Trucks 4

At Work 16

Glossary 22
Read More 23
Internet Sites 23
Index 24

About Dump Trucks

Look!

Here comes a dump truck.

Count the big tires.

This dump truck has six.

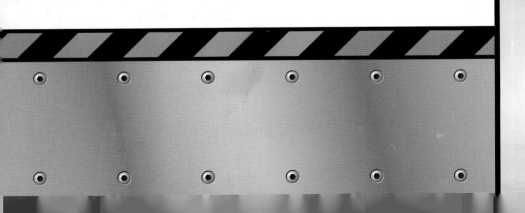

See the dump box?

It holds the load.

dump box

Here is the back of
the dump box.
It is called the gate.

CONSTRUCTION VEHICLE

gate

The driver moves a lever.

Up goes the dump box.

The gate opens.

The dirt falls out.

At Work

Dump trucks carry
away big rocks.

Dump trucks bring in gravel.

The gravel spills out.

Workers build a new road.

Good job, dump truck!

Glossary

gate—the part at the back of a truck that opens and closes; the gate is also called a tailgate

gravel—loose rocks

lever—a bar inside the cab of a dump truck that a driver uses to raise and lower the dump box

load—what is carried by the dump truck

Read More

Hayes, Amy. *Big Dump Trucks.* Machines that Work. New York: Cavendish Square Publishing, 2016.

Lennie, Charles. *Dump Trucks.* Construction Machines. Minneapolis: Abdo Kids, 2015.

Osier, Dan. *Dump Trucks.* Construction Site. New York: PowerKids Press, 2014.

Internet Sites

FactHound offers a safe, fun way to find Internet sites related to this book. All of the sites on FactHound have been researched by our staff.

Here's all you do:
Visit *www.facthound.com*
Type in this code: 9781515725268

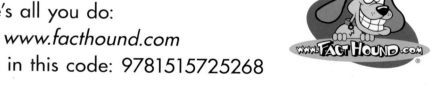

 Super-cool stuff! Check out projects, games and lots more at **www.capstonekids.com**

Index

dirt, 14

drivers, 12

dump box, 8, 10, 12

gate, 10, 14

gravel, 18

levers, 12

loads, 8

roads, 20

rocks, 16

tires, 6

workers, 20